M

MY TALK WITH GOD

*How can we talk about life and not talk about children;
babies?*

*How can we say we want to save the world but yet the
element and elements of life is not honoured by fathers
and mothers?*

*How can we say we love life, but yet cannot give our
children the basic necessities of life?*

*So what is life to you God?
What is life to man; humans?*

What is the meaning of life?

Michelle and Michelle Jean

It's amazing how we say we love, but yet in all of our love, we leave all in disarray.

We have children and cannot feed them, cannot honour them by doing that which is right, fair and just for them.

Mama and daddy ignore them; abandon them.
The government ignores them.
Leave them in hostels and or government homes where they are mistreated, abused, molested and left for dead.

The government say they care, but they care not for them.
Care not if they live or die.

Care not for their welfare and well being. As long as these children are kept from society that is all that matters. They have mental issues; are born with deformities.

None of these government officials think that it could be their child from their loins that have to suffer this fate.

They don't think that as government officials that oversee and govern the land, these children belongs to them; are their own flesh and blood because they took an oath when they went into office to protect and provide for all.

These governments don't think or see that a part of the problem is them; the genetically modified and inorganic food they allow farmers and manufacturers to manipulate and produce; feed their own people.

These government officials don't think that in all they do in office they are judged for their sinful actions here on this earth.

They don't think of the well being of their land and people. All they think about is their own greed and inhumane way of doing things; governing their land and people.

So now Good God, because right now you are no longer Lovey, you are only God and Good God. You are no longer the Breath of Life; Allelujah because in truth, true and Good Life is not unjust but just.

Yes I am coming to you this way not in doubt but in dismay as to what I saw on the internet.

No not Lovey, but God. What is beauty to man; humans?

Is beauty flesh or is beauty the goodness that we do that radiates through the spirit?

You know what Lovey; I can't do this because I cannot get far without calling you Lovey. So it's back to Lovey I go. Lovey is more appropriate and you will not let me continue on with God or Good God. Respect is due and I have to truly give you respect. So I ask you again, what is beauty?

What is beauty and or true beauty in your eyes Lovey?

Is beauty flesh or is beauty the goodness of spirit that radiates from inner to outer and from outer to inner?

I know our sins make us ugly.

I know environmental cleanliness and the lack thereof of it makes us ugly; well dirty our spirit and make us old in many ways. Thus earth is severely polluted and man; different governments squabble about rectifying the problem.

Lovey, please tell me what's going on with humanity and the way they treat children?

I know it's hard but how can a woman have a child and just abandon them like that?

How can a woman feel so much pain and just dump a child in a garbage bin just like that?

Yes I know there are underlying and or underlining psychological issues, but this is a child Lovey. To me if you don't want children do not have any. You do not punish a person if they don't want to have children come on now.

If you cannot handle one do not have a second one. Children are not always a blessing. Some are hell on wheels.

Some don't even give a crap about you as parents.

Look at my struggles raising mine. Where were the fathers in all of this for the long haul? Was it not you Lovey that stood with me throughout my storms and still standing with me despite me saying I want to leave you?

Men tell us children are a blessing, but if you cannot take care of your child, how are they a blessing?

Tell me Lovey, how are children a blessing when as parents we cannot truly take care of them.

Tell me, how are children a blessing when we have to bug the government to help us take care of them? Did the government lay with us to have them? ***So why do we pressure the government for children we did not think of before we had them?*** *Yes this is a double standard on my part because the government is also wrong. Do not say you are going to help parents with their children; special needs children and truly do not help them.*

Do not allow people to abuse them because these children are our future; the future builders and prospectors of our country; the land we call home.

Men want kids, but look at the statistics Lovey. How many of them cut out on their child and or children?

How many have and has abandoned them?

How many of them have and has shun their responsibilities as a father?

So tell me Lovey, **WHAT GOOD IS A MAN THAT CANNOT TRULY LOVE AND PROVIDE FOR THEIR BIOLOGICAL AND SPIRITUAL OWN?**

So tell me, how is a child a blessing when mama and daddy abandons them; leave them broken and unfed; unwanted?

As our father, do you not do the same to us, your chosen?

Do we not feel abandoned and unwanted by you?

How many have shed tears; cried out in pain and suffering to you, and you do not hear them? Yes I know not all in life has and have chosen you, but I've chosen you and you've left me in pain all around; broken.

Do I not trust you to stand by my children as their grandfather and father and you've let me down?

Don't you dare say it because it does hurt to hear my child say he does not believe in you because you do not help.

Lovey we all have our demons including you, but no child should have to say that to you if a parent has and have dedicated them to your good and true service. Yes I know we do not do this before conception but I learnt my mistake the hard way, but I am not giving up hope that one day, all will be alright for me and them including the good and true seeds you've given me.

Some children are born with deformities and illness. And I commend these parents that stick it out with their children because I know how hard it is to raise your child that is sick and or have disabilities.

Oh man the saying is true. Anyone can be a dad, but it takes a real man and a real woman to raise that child. There are challenges trust me and we have to face them despite the pain and hardship (s) that face us. Thus give yourself a hug if you are going through the struggles and pain like me. You are strong and you will make it. Be proud of you and hold your head and hand up and give thanks. You made it. Lovey is there for you and he's carrying you through. Yes I know you feel he's not there but he is there right beside you. He's holding your hand because if it wasn't for him, you don't know where you might be today.

So for all of you that are in doubt, trust me, there is absolutely no punishment for not wanting children.

Now I come to this Lovey. In the book of death; man's so called Holy Book it is written where you said, to be fruitful and multiply, but you know what Lovey; I am so going to leave this alone because I know creation; what the first human looked like. This knowledge cannot change and it will stand for all generations to come more than indefinitely. Until I see otherwise, **_I will leave this alone because the creation of male and female was good; blessed but when it came to the forming of man; then your actions in the book of sin; man's so called Holy Bible as to forming man; they were not blessed, nor where they good._**

Thus good people are created and evil is formed.

Thus we have two levels of life. That which you created and that which were formed from the earth. Meaning there is a spiritual and physical life. As humans we have both thus we have a choice. If you are good, you are from the collective of good; good spirits. They guide and protect you, thus they can control your spirit; meaning stop you from walking on the pathway of evil.

Yes I know this is not the best explanation I can give Lovey. I know what I am talking about but yet it's difficult to explain.

Creation cannot change because all of creation were and still is good. There is no evil in creation because all of creation was and still is blessed and if humans read properly they would see this in Genesis 1. Thus the separation of good and evil; those that were created and those who are formed for Mother Earth herself.

When men were formed from the dust of the earth, you did not say man was good, nor did you say you blessed man.

One man was formed from the dust of the earth in Genesis 2 but in Genesis 1 according to man's Holy Book you said, "Let us make man in our image, after our likeness..."

So Lovey, who were you speaking to when you said in accordance to man's holy book, "Let us?"

Who is this us? When I saw the formation of life out of the darkness, I saw nothing else within that darkness. I saw no one standing around or above this darkness. All I felt was this peace and calm. Thus I said, if man saw what I saw, they would not sin. I have never felt this peace and calm in my human life Lovey, but yet I felt it for the very first time. When you see such beauty and feel such calm, who would want to walk amongst evil. Life is truly beautiful but yet we as humans destroy it and you let us.

This I cannot fully comprehend.

I witnessed the birth of life with my own eyes (spiritual eye) Lovey. So tell me why do humans not want this?

I saw the first man and he was black. So why is there such a dispute on earth when it comes to humans; black people in hue. Did you not form and or create the first human in hue black?

I told humanity what he looked like. Yes humanity especially the white race and or other races will dispute this, but I truly do not care Lovey. They can dispute all they want, but they cannot change that which is done; recorded in the record books of time; physical and spiritual history; truth. You saw it befitting to show me the truth and this truth cannot change because it is written in our books also.

Now I need to know how evil came about and you are locking this off from me. I need to know all Lovey; thus I need to tell humanity how evil came about and why we as the black race chose evil over good long before the Ethiopians of old sold you out.

There is more to this Lovey, hence I seek your full and true knowledge. You cannot keep us in the dark when it comes to the full truth. I am ready for this Lovey. I am ready for the unconditional truth. You owe us as humanity this much. All we've had are lies of people that wanted to keep us from you. The more we sin is the more we die; meaning the longer our spirit stay in jail in hell and burn before the eventual extinction of our spirit.

Yes the wages of sin is death. But Lovey, if you strip a man woman or child of his or her birthright, what will they have left?

Will they not worship the gods and idols of the ones that strip their birthright from them?

Is this not what the black community globally has and have done?

Was the birthright of the black community globally not stripped and or taken from them?

Do we as blacks know you?

Do we not worship and praise other gods. Gods we think are you and are truly not?

Yes I know this book has changed from where I started but you need to see life. I know you cannot see life on my level because you are far more superior. But in truth, you need to start healing our pain. I've tried to heal yours but I truly cannot. I don't think I am the right person to do this. Also, you are not telling me how to truly help you to heal you.

Like I said in the previous book to this; no one should say they do not believe in you because you do not help them.

I shouldn't do it and my children shouldn't do it either. Yes I know knowledge is the key, but if we do not have true knowledge of you, how can we choose you?

The time of evil is over, but yet things are not happening for evil to leave. Yes I know I am impatient.

Yes it's ya think. I just want everything that is evil to be gone right away so that our chosen; well your chosen globally can truly live.

I keep seeking and I'm being kept from finding my true place with you.

I don't know Lovey because you like it when I get mad at you it seems.

Fam and people; my true family, I don't know this morning because it's a new day. The lines above were written September 12, 2015 and it's now September 13th and now I am totally confused.

Fam and people; my true family, you know how I want to leave Lovey right. But you know Lovey is not going to let me leave him because of the true bond that we have. Well this morning I had some really weird dreams and Fam I want to be a hypocrite. I want to bury what I am seeing. I want to hide what I am seeing from you. See I tell White People where they came from. I cuss them out and tell them the truth of them, but when it comes to my own black people excluding Babylonians; I want to hide what I am seeing from them. I truly don't the world, not truly, but I don't want to world to know this and or get a bad picture of us. There are so many stereotypes and negative feelings out there towards us that I don't want these dreams now to be common place; send a bad or evil picture of us. Thus the hypocrisy in me. I've told you in some of my other books; earlier stages of books that I refuse to lie to any of you. You are my true family and I will not give you lies nor will I tell you lies. Thus I am telling you of my feel, what I want to do. But I refuse to concede to the negative side of me because as blacks we are definitely not perfect and some of us are pure and constant evil. Not everyone in the Black Race or Community belongs to Lovey. FROM YOU ABANDON LOVEY, IT'S BYE BYE BYE FOR YOU and we saw this with Ethiopia and other African Nations until this day. **_Once you leave the fold of Lovey and depending on what you did for him to dismiss and or eject you from his fold, it is virtually impossible for you to get back in._** Some people cannot get back in no matter how hard they try. Just ask Eve (Evening) and Satan. Trust me it's not easy and once you are locked out, you are locked out more than indefinitely. This is why I tell you to know your sins. If you have converted willingly to Islam you had better keep walking because you will never ever get back into Lovey's realm.

Yes I know the lifeline that is given to those blacks who have converted to Islam without know the full truth of Islam. You have a lifeline because you truly did not know. Thus it is **BLACK DEVIL'S THAT THE DEVIL AND OR SATAN USE TO DRAW US OUT.** Thus hell is full of black people and recruiting more. No true Jew can walk in the fold of this cult of murderers. If you've converted to this cult of liars, deceivers and murderers and you want to make right with Lovey, truly beg Lovey forgiveness and walk away from this cult in peace if you value your physical and spiritual life.

Thus Ethiopia lie to humanity by saying they have the Ark of the Covenant when they truly do not. They don't even know what the Ark of the Covenant is. Ethiopia lost their place indefinitely with Lovey and there is no way in hell can they return to his fold. Trust me he has more than a bone to pick with this land.

Some blacks are demons thus I will not sugar coat anything nor will I lie to you despite my feel.

I cannot give one race what I see of them and when it comes to black people hide what I see of them.

I am not here to judge thus we as black people are no exception to the rule. We must know of our ugly past as well. I saw some different dreams this morning. Some I can remember but some I truly cannot because they are vague. Thus I have to wonder about our <u>CHILDREN OF THE GLOBE.</u>

I have to wonder why Lovey permit us to have children that we cannot take care of. <u>HAVE TO WONDER WHAT BE FRUITFUL AND MULTIPLY REALLY MEANS TO HIM; US?</u>

Many things I wonder; ponder about in my head and it's him Lovey that I must go to for truth; all that confuses me.

I talked to him about evil and what I saw. The darkness giving birth to blue and white thus the heavens as we call it (sky for some) was the first to be given birth. But yet, as I think about this event and how peace and calm I felt, I have to wonder even ponder if this event is true evil. I am confused because I truly do not get the Blue and White; thus the dominance of these two colours here on earth. I am not getting something and this concerns me. It baffles me because I felt the true peace and calm of the birth of these two colours. So if something is truly this peaceful and calm, why am I speculating about it?

Why do I associate good and evil with it; more evil than good?

Am I that clueless and lacking knowledge that I would associate this birth with evil?

I know blue and white is dependent on each other. We as humans need these two colours in order to survive I guess.

Yes some of you say they are reflective colours but in truth they are not reflective colours they are true. Hence they are true to the darkness because the darkness gave them to us. They are colours of light because the light needs them for balance in many ways. We as humans need them also. So what am I missing Lovey because I truly do not know.

*Certain things are hard for me hence I must give it time; true time. I will find the truth; true truth one day, so I have to let my confusion go and free myself. **As I told you this morning, evil cannot change and will never change. I told*** *you, NO ONE SHOULD WANT TO CHANGE THE NEXT PERSON.*

Evil do all to change you and assimilate you into their environment and this is wrong. **No one should have to give up their right to accept another man's wrong.**

If you are wrong you are wrong. I cannot give you right for the wrongs that you have done. Thus I keep telling you, **GOOD PEOPLE SHOULD NOT HAVE TO SUFFER FOR THE EVILS OF THE NEXT MAN AND OR PERSON.** *When you continue to let this happen Lovey you are wrong. I will not give you right for the wrongs you have done.* **NO WRONG CAN BE RIGHT, and it's time for us as humans to stop living wrong because our wrongs do take us to hell.** *We are punished for those wrongs and that punishment is death. But before the spirit dies, it must face hell's fire; ovens and or cylinder pits.*

Thus truly listen to CHANGES by Pac; Tupac because his words are truly true. Therefore, I know the threats of evil. **When wicked and evil people KNOW THAT YOU ARE INFLUENTIAL THEY DO ALL TO ELIMINATE YOU, especially if you are black.**

Evil cannot change, but if you are good and true to self, truly love you, you can make positive changes for you.

Once you begin to make positive changes for you, over time people will see and make changes for self and others no matter how small that change is.

Goodness does not strive to change you.

Goodness is always good.

Goodness will never seek the good in you. Why should goodness do that?

If you are good you are good and people will see the goodness in you.

Thus I do not seek to change anyone, nor will I do to change you. Your beliefs are your beliefs and I cannot go against my truth. You must know what your truths are.

Some people are true to good and true life and some people are true to death. This is the reality of life because there is good and evil and we see this each and every day.

My truths are not your truths because we do not share the same values, nor do we share the same creator; Lovey and or ancestry; roots.

In all that evil does, evil do all to eliminate all that is good.

Evil believe they can live free here on earth when all good is gone. **_But what evil do not realize is that good maintains the balance of this world. We are the ones that keep this earth rotating. We maintain the eco system._**

But earth is dying.

Yes the earth is dying for man; humans.

Yes earth's eco system is off balance I know. But that is because of sin and the greed of man; men and woman that do not see the value and beauty of earth; their surroundings. So as Mama continues to be unbalanced so will man be. Meaning, earth must align herself for the destruction of man; billions on a global scale. How would you say. Oh man this is hard because we were the ones to shift the clock of life towards death if that makes any sense.

So no, I cannot hide this truth from you because in some of my earlier books I did tell you that I was seeing ugly black men. There is an ugliness that surrounds black men and I am seeing it more and more. I cannot hide this from us as a people or anyone. So into my dreams I go.

This morning I was dreaming about magazines. Two particular magazines. I believe one said PnG enterprise, no, not enterprise. I can't remember the last name but if it comes to me, I will let you know at the end of this book or in another book. And it was definitely PnG. I am going to check Google Images to see if I can find the logo. So please, no one sue me because I am trying to show you what I saw. The name of the other magazine I cannot remember but the lady that ran and or operated PnG was black and skinny. People OMG because her colour was greyish. Greyish is how I can describe her. Oh dear lord she was skinny and her skin was drooping. She was ugly. I will try to find a picture on Google Images to show you what I am talking about. The black models in her company was beautiful and skinny and of a lighter chocolate hue with straight hair. None had nappy hair like mine.

*Hence in the dream I said we must have more black magazines. **The highlight of these magazines were not the models but the skinniness and ugliness of this woman.***

People and Fam, I know sins eat us out and make us ugly. For me to be seeing this ugliness more and more and reflected as black is beyond me.

In my other dream, I dreamt I was driving on the highway. My niece called me and I told her I was heading to Brampton. I had to meet my son. Driving I passed tractor trailers heading in the opposite direction. What was odd about the dream was that she lived on the highway. Her house along with other people's homes were in the middle of the highway. No not middle. The highway then was built around the homes almost in a triangle and she was at the end of the triangle that had English and Hindi and or Bangladeshi and or Pakistani writing. No she wasn't at the end or tip of the triangle. I stopped at the end and or the tip of the triangle because I passed her house. At the tip and or end of the triangle Hindi and or Pakistani and or Bangladeshi language encapsulated the English words. Reaching the end of the triangle I realized I missed my niece's home and I had to turn back. I didn't turn back but someone came to get me. This young black girl that was in her early and or late twenties dressed in this green dress came to meet me. The green dress she was wearing clung to her and you could see her butt that was well rounded in the dress. She wore a g-string I believe, but it was her well rounded nice butt that you saw. Yes I am jumping ahead of my dream. Before I got to the tip and or end of the triangle, about mid way where the triangle starts to become tiny, I saw my niece's mother. I think she was at a window and in gold and red. Do not quote me on the red but gold and or yellow she had on. I was telling her while driving something bad is going to happen. I am not 100% sure if I said something bad is going to happen to Canada and or in this country. But I know I told her something bad is going to happen to humanity real soon. She knew of this destruction and she held up her hand as if she was going to get into the spirit like some of us black people do. White people your spiritualism is different from ours thus our praise and worship is truly different from yours. You don't get black spiritualism nor do we get yours.

What struck me odd about my niece's mom was her straight nose and short hair that was white like paper. She looked older and I said to myself in the dream, how come she looked so old and has all grey hair. Family and people, my true family, she had not one black hair on her head. Now to catch up, the young black girl came to get me and I described her to you. Family and People, the lead she was leading me to my niece's home, there was pure dog dodo everywhere in the grass. I had to jump over the dodo not to step in it. Dear God it was disgusting. When I got to her home it was a mess. Mess everywhere and this young black guy was in her house. People and Family, the guy was just sitting there watching television and not doing anything. Yu noa dem man wey freeload and just mooch affa yu fi everything. Well a demday type a man disya man was. All out lazy. I don't know what happened people but apparently I got some cooked shrimp in my hand and I was eating the shrimp. I had some of the skin or shell in my hand and I threw the shell and or skin in the garbage, but the shell and or skin ended up on her bed that was ¾ spread. I had to ask the same girl that retrieved me to take up the shells and or skin for me and she did. There were children in the room and one particular child had a bit of her hair on one side of her head shaved and the other part of her head, her hair was cane rowed down but it needed to be redone because it was messy. I told her school is starting in a couple of days, why isn't her hair done and my niece took her hair out. People this little black girl had the longest natural hair. That was the end of that dream. Did I miss something with this dream?

Yes.

Before I got into my nieces home, she had 2 dogs outside and one black one caged and tied up. I had a dog with me and this dog that was caged saw my dog and wanted to attack it but he was caged. Upon rushing his cage my niece's dogs went on the attack but my dog held them back.

Was there poop?

Yes.

Family and people I know this is a dream inna dream. One part had to do with my son and the other part has to do with my niece.

I know my niece is seeing someone that I not working; lazy. I don't know if he's left her home because a booty call to him is an invitation to stay. You are a booty call not a mainstay so truly leave.

Anyway fam, I am so not going to get wrapped up in this because I know shit is all around my niece and inside of her home is dirty. I cannot comprehend why my niece keep getting into messes that's hard for her to come out of. She has children and they should be her priority not some lazy ass shirt that cannot help her nor help build her in life.

I am so tired of her booty calls. Learn to bleeping abstain for God sake man come on now. You cannot be a bleeping romping shop and or room for men. Control your damn urges that get you in trouble.

I don't know fam because sex should not be a priority for anyone. No, I should not say that. Not because I am not having any. Sex and the art of making love is truly beautiful with the right someone and when it takes fold beauty happens. I know this but you cannot have booty calls with this man and that man all the time. It's not becoming. Wait until you find the right someone. I don't care if a man wears a condom his scent is still on you. Give yourself and your body time before you get involved with another man.

It is truly nasty for us as humans to run from disya man ya to datdey one ya and so forth. As humans we do stink because we carry odour and bacteria. Everyone's scent is different thus think. Some woman and man do not smell pretty. I know when I write certain damaging books and I sweat my odour is not pretty. It's high thus the changes in my body for real.

Our body odour can get so high that other's smell it even if you wear deodorant. I know this because my son have and has told me mom your armpits wreak; is that high. So as males and females we have to know our body changes because it does change.

When we incorporate another person's odour with us and or in us and or on us, our odour changes as well. Some woman and men do not smell good and our downstairs won't smell good as well. I know this for a fact especially if the man have multiple partners. Many of us don't realize this. I never learnt this fully until later on in life. So it's imperative to know how your man smell around you.

I know we as females undergo body changes thus our odour changes with our cycle; menstrual cycle. What I am saying is, know your body. If you are done with a man or woman, give your body time to heal; well get rid of their odour.

As for my niece, I will not get involved in her shit and bullshit because I am tired of talking to her thus I do not call her. She's changed her number and has a new one for which she gave to me and I just I put down; will have to search for it if I need to call her.

I swear this girl has loser radar stamped on her.
She keeps meeting these losers that are not there for her. Thus the using game is coming right back around. So I have to leave her alone to deal with her own mess and messes.

She's a grown woman and she needs to know where her priorities lie. She makes these messes and no matter how I *talk, she keeps going back into them and I have to leave her alone now. I have my own issues to deal with so I can't concern myself with her because she too do not listen.*

Yu talk to har bout di same thing and she keep going back into them. Suh a fi har wataloo.

This dream is strange because I dreamt about David Geffen. He was in black and the black jacket he was wearing had gold markings on it. Water, cloudy water was around him because he was doing an interview I guess but you could not see the interviewer. He went into the water with his nice black jacket and he was saying at the bottom of the water and or tank and or his fish sanctuary there were sharks. You could not see the sharks nor could you see any fishes. People and Fam, my true family, when the man emerged from the water it was as if his jacket did not get wet. He came out of the water like I said and walked towards me and I saw this old black man that was thin with a little hump and or lump in his back. It was as if his skin was decaying, being eaten. Walking towards me he was no longer in black but in this grey suit and his shoulders were broad. Fam and people, my true family, this man was so ugly, oh God I want to vomit now as to what I saw.

So Lovey truly tell me, is grey death; the state of being your spirit becomes before you die?

So Fam and people you know the reason why I wanted to withhold this information from you in humanity. This ugliness. Yes it's beyond me but I have to figure it out.

Yes I am confused because when evil dies especially if you are black, you die as a white person dressed in white.

Now I am seeing white death on a different level. When you; some of you are about to die and or dying, you die in grey and your skin turns grey and ugly and you look like a black person.

Shit, sorry, man is death confusing. What do I call this type of death Lovey?

Are you trying to tell me that there are different levels of death? **SO BLACK IS WHITE AND WHITE IS BLACK WHEN IT COMES TO CERTAIN DEATH.** *Strange.*

This is new and confusing to me. Thus death masks death for real literally.

The PnG I am looking for is not on the internet. Hey maybe this has nothing to do with beautiful black models but has all to do with the head of PnG who knows.

This is the best image I can find on the internet that represent the woman I was talking about. Her legs were like her hands and more drooping; soggy. She was skinnier than the woman in this picture with greyish skin. Picture used for illustration purposes and no copyright infringement intended.

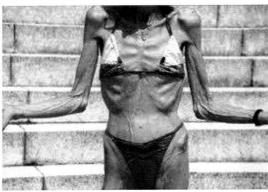

*As humans we cannot tell another person what beauty is if you do not know true beauty. No one should tell you to be this way or that way. We are all of different shapes and sizes; body type and it's not fair for someone to come in and say the ideal weight for humans is 120 pounds. We cannot all be 120 pounds. You as an individual cannot starve yourself to death **TO PLEASE SOMEONE ELSE AND OR YOUR FALSE PERCEPTION OF BEAUTY.** Beauty radiates from inner to outer and from outer to inner and this all has to do with your good and true deeds, not flesh.*

*Society has and have become obsessed with beauty that we say false beauty is beauty. **The false beauty and or beauty that you buy cannot change what your child grow up to look like. Meaning the beauty that you buy to*** _**deceive others cannot change your spiritual DNA, nor can it change your physical DNA.**_

Ugly will always be ugly. Thus the ugliness of our sins do come back to haunt us.

ALWAYS BE YOU AND DON'T CHANGE YOU TO PLEASE THE NEXT PERSON. IF THAT PERSON TRULY CARES FOR YOU AND TRULY LOVES YOU, HE OR SHE WOULD NOT WANT YOU TO CHANGE YOU.

If you are a chubby chaser, chase that chubby woman and truly love her.

If you are a skinny jean chaser, chase that skinny jean and truly love her.

My preference and acceptance in not yours, so don't impose your views on me. _I live in a real world not an unrealistic one where people do all to control and dominate each other. If this is your world; stay the hell out of mine because you are rejected; will never be accepted._

You are not a part of my good and true world.

Life, good and true life has nothing to do with lies, it has all to do with truth; everlasting life.

Many of you do not want everlasting life; so you lie to others by accepting all that is false whilst thinking your falseness is true beauty.

Yes I get down on Lovey because I truly do not comprehend why we as black people have to become ugly. **But it's not we as black people that are ugly; it's white people that becomes ugly to the point where you want to vomit. THUS HUE IN THE PHYSICAL WORLD AND SENSE IS TRULY UGLY.**

And yes this is why LOVEY DO NOT BASE THINGS ON AND OR OFF HUE. ONLY HUMANS DO THIS BECAUSE HUMANS DO NOT KNOW THE VALUE AND BEAUTY OF TRUTH; THEIR TRUE SELF.

OUR SINS HAVE AND HAS MADE US UGLY. SO YES, THERE IS BEAUTY AND UGLINESS AND DARKNESS IN US AS BLACK PEOPLE AND WHITE PEOPLE. MAYBE THIS IS WHAT LOVEY HAS BEEN TRYING TO SHOW ME.

NOT BECAUSE WE ARE BLACK DOES THAT MAKE US GOOD. NOT BECAUSE WE ARE WHITE DOES THAT MAKE US GOOD.
So no, I will not hide the ugliness of black and white people because at the end of the

day, we all sin; thus the ugliness of sin in all of us in humanity.

I will not sugar coat anything because Lovey did not tell me to sugar coat anything.

I will not lie for the black race or for any race for that matter. We did sin AND WE DID BECOME UGLY. WE LET THE UGLINESS OF SIN IN THUS MAKING US; SELF, UNCLEAN; DIRTY.

*The colour black was never dirty, we as black people and white people dirtied it. Like I said, we allowed sin into our domain; lives. **Thus black has nothing to do with hue because like I said, WHITES ARE BLACKS TOO AND THEY TOO HAVE DIRTIED SELF. SO AS I LAMBASTE BLACKS WHITES ARE LAMBASTED ALSO BECAUSE THEY TOO ARE ONE OF US; FALL UNDER THE BANNER OF BLACK.***

Yes I know not all and it's not all blacks that fall under the banner of black. Hence it's time we as black people whether white or black in hue; stop the bullshit of letting evil into our lives. Babylonians you are not a part of this thus you are not included. Your god and gods are yours therefore, you have no place in Lovey's world and kingdom, nor do you have a place in mine.

This is the language I saw wrapped around English words.

And no people, I am so not going to give you a history lesson on this language nor do I want and need to.

This language concern me not, thus what do not concern me I truly leave it alone.

The black man's god and or the black race god is not the god and gods of Babylon; thus our original language, hair, culture, heritage, being, songs, dress, way of living is truly not like theirs, nor will it ever be for the true black race.

The days of old is not the days of today to me. Thus we will never ever be assimilated in their race ever again.

Humanity is going to face their trials and tribulations real soon yes because humanity as we know it will never ever be the same again.

Billions are going to become extinct and there is nothing. Absolutely nothing humans globally can do about this. We caused this upon ourselves thus the death and destruction of self; humans globally. All that we were not to do we did. We disobeyed the laws of life and now its payment time. We must pay for the consequences of our actions.

Like I've said in some of my other books; ole people sey, if you caane get quakoo yu mus get shut. SO SATAN AND OR EVIL AND OR THE DEVIL COULD NOT GET TO LOVEY, SO INSTEAD HE GOT TO HIS CHILDREN.

So if you cannot get daddy you must get his kids and or someone around him even if it is a good friend.

This is what the triangle looked like that the highway went by and or surrounded.

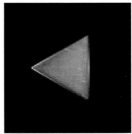

So you have a full idea of the dream. As for the dream with David Geffen, I cannot find a image that closely resemble the black man he turned into.

Yes it's sad that in our lives we cannot see the sins that we do. Thus the ugliness of spirit; the ugly spirit in us that we cannot see.

Man do I need natural beauty. Thus I have to seek out the comforts of nature all around.

I am tired of the fake hair; weave crap that we as black people wear too. Why can we truly love our natural and nappy hair?

Tell me, why is it that we do not find our own hair beautiful? There is so much that we can do with it but yet we truly do not invest in styling our own hair naturally.

Man I so have to cut mine. Too long thus the short hair is so for me. People wow, I admire people with full white hair; grey hair as we call it.

Fam and people, this hair is so gorgeous and I can't wait until mine fully turn paper white. But I doubt if it will because the back of my hair refuses to grey thus my salt and pepper hair.

It doesn't bother me sometimes because at times it feels as if I have no hair on my head. Soon I will cut it because I can't take the dead hair. No, I don't fuss with my hair so if you have naturally long black hair then truly take care of it naturally.

Keep the chemicals and dyes away from your hair.

Michelle and Michelle Jean.

There isn't much I want to talk about, but this is me on given days.

Oh I don't know if this is relevant or not but I can't remember if I saw the full destruction of earth in the living. Oh well I am so not going to worry about this because if Lovey had wanted me to remember I would have.

And please do not ask me about this white lady in white because I truly do not know who she is. I do not know what relevance she has in the spiritual world. Thus when she comes to me fully then I will know.

People and family, my true family call me stupid but are scientists missing something?

Maybe I am wrong and I am reading into this stupidly. But maybe this was what Lovey was showing me with the Air France disappearing in the sky. **Maybe scientists need to look at the African and Arabian Tectonic Plates, the Caribbean and the Cocos Tectonic Plates.**

Oh my God, is this the dream I had with Shaggy?

Dear God what are you saying to me and what are you trying to tell me? Are you telling me these regions are going to split apart shortly?

Dear God am I right because my insides are panicking?

Lovey, is this the major destruction and separation?

Dear God the world truly won't be the same. This is the cost of our sins thus Mother Africa asked for prayer literally and she was given prayer.

Thus Africa must separate from Eurasia and South America must separate from North America.

Lovey I truly don't know. Maybe I am going mad at what I am seeing here.

But then again; my thinking is not on the normal level of man; humanity as a whole. What I see they cannot see, so it matters not if they call me a crack pot that has gone mad and insane.

So Lovey, how powerful is this destruction going to be because I saw the detonation in Nevada and I could not save there?

Michelle and Michelle Jean

My thoughts are all over the place Lovey because confusion is setting in. I cannot over stand why you would allow so much sin to take place here on earth.

I get it with the choice, but with getting it with the choice, why not keep everything good in the first place?

Why let sin escape and do so much damage?

I do not get it with the heavens. And in some way, this is a lie on my part. I did watch twincredibles and behind the facade, I feel and see the animosity. I get it but I truly do not get it on another level.

Thus I have to ask, are we born with jealousy?

No, jealousy is learnt in many ways. I don't know Lovey because something is truly not right and my mind is swirling here and there right now.

Dreams are confusing because my son was talking to me about Gotham City and the Joker and I ended up dreaming about Robin and these intelligent creatures that was fighting. Thus my sci-fi dream world I am so going to leave alone because my dream world is truly weird like me.

Also dreamt I was fighting. These young black youths were sitting on the block and one of them who was not supporting his child was abusing his baby mamma. I don't know Lovey because the dream is weird. The little boy did not want any confusion, but in the dream after some commotion and confusion, I figured out that the youth that was abusing the young lady were related and he fathered a child. The little boy was his child. So I got mad and blurted out that he fathered a child with his own family member. He did not like that and he tapped his waist to say he was packing and I should be careful. I told him he did not scare me and I had my crew. Thinking my crew had my back I called for them and none showed up. I was on my own and trust me I whooped his ass physically.

Lovey, I don't even know why I bother with black people in my dream world. They never have my back. My fight is not our fight. They leave my ass alone because my fight is not their fight. I can fix it and help myself, so they leave me alone all the time. Powerless and worthless are they in the spiritual realm when it comes to true help. They don't know you; well at least me any way.

It's like they are happy and content with the crap they are being fed. It's like I am not with you and never will be with you. Damn are we conformist.

I guess in the dream world what don't concern them they truly leave it alone. Damn.

I don't concern them so they leave me alone.

The full truth does not concern them so they truly leave it alone. Weird

So as I am left helpless in the spiritual realm by my own black men, it's the same in the physical world. They leave my ass alone.

Oh man, I need a true vacation. People, I truly do not know what these dreams mean, so I am so going to leave them alone. This one though is not a dream. I got up to use the bathroom and I could not get back to sleep. I closed my eyes and I saw Wesley Snipes in a dead position before me. It was like he was lying in a casket dead. Trust me I could not lose his face. My true family and people, I truly do not know what these waking state visions mean. So I put no value to them. I just toss them under junk and leave them alone because they are meaningless to me.

Oh man I can't think because something is truly not right here on earth.

I can't figure out death anymore nor can I figure out life. I cannot get over why Lovey would allow chaos to be unleashed here on earth for so long.

*We are all human beings but it seems Lovey do not value life. **IT'S LIKE MAN AS IN MALES CREATE THIS MESS AND WE AS FEMALES HAVE TO COME IN AND FIX THE MESS THEY'VE CAUSED.***

Thus man as in males will always abandon females to do their dirty works while they just sit around and take credit for it all.

Lovey, is this not like you?

All your chosen are females and we are the ones that have to fix your mess. Why?

Why create faulty in the first place?

If all was so good, would goodness not reign supreme always?

If you were true to you and your people, would you not give good and true?

Would you not create and build so that no evil can and or will get in?

If you blessed your creation in the first stage of life, why are we living amongst evil and wicked people?

Would you not have secured a good and true place for us where no evil and sin could enter?

Would you not have sealed your good and true people with your protection of goodness and truth so that no evil could sway them and let them stray from you?

Would you have not built impenetrable frameworks and foundations around them; your good and true people?

So in all of this Lovey, you too do not make sense to me. You don't willing aide the females in your life. Thus men can walk over us and say we are inferior, lowly and we are not counted.

So tell me, what kind of crap you created and call it humane; human?

What is humanity to you?

What is creating good and true to you?

Why create man; males to rule; control and dominate?

Why have dominion over all Lovey, when humans cannot control self; meaning live right and true; good by you and self?

Are you as Lovey, Good God and Allelujah not flawed then?

So you as God; Lovey are not without flaws because you do create faulty.

I don't know Lovey, but you have to bare the burden and pain for some of this. Like I've told you, you are not without fault. You too are to blame for some of the mess on earth and you are going to have to fix it. As God you cannot pawn off your responsibilities on someone else. You did wrong and you are to make amends for your wrongs also.

I've told you, if all we are given is sin, we will do sinful things and we will become sinful.

If we are given sacrifices Lovey all the days of our lives, we will come to make sacrifices unto other gods, animals and what have you.

*Some people make sacrifices by killing animals and humans and you are okay with this and this is wrong. **You cannot give false and expect us to live by the truth.***

Over the course of history you've allowed men to give us false hope.

You've allowed men and women to teach us wrong.

You've allowed senseless killings.

You've allowed the rape and abuse of the young and elderly and this is wrong.

*You've allowed this earth to be in disarray without truly fixing it. And this is wrong on your part. Things are broken on earth **and the earth not just humans** need to be fixed.*

Evil surrounds us and kill us all. And in all you've done, you have not truly separated good from evil more than indefinitely. So tell me now Lovey, how can we have compassion for you when you have no compassion for self and us; your good and true people?

You cannot say you love us so and let us continue to live in filth. We can no longer dirty ourselves with evil; wicked and evil people that have no good will for others. When you continue to do this Lovey, you are no different from evil. You are telling us that you truly don't care and this is truly wrong on your part. If we have no abiding city with you, how can we abide with you?

If a father and mother don't care, how are they expecting their children to care?

Like I've said, my dream world is changing and I cannot change it. The dreams are getting weird and you see that from above.

I am also dreaming about Russia again. I dreamt I was in this place in Russia where all old people and or older people (seniors) reside. I was given this black hard cover book that was about 8 1/2 by 14 cm if not a bit longer. The names of people (these older people that I was amongst) were written in this book. In the book beside each person's name was a cheque. I cannot tell you the amount of the cheque because I did not see a figure on the cheques. It's like the Government of Russia gave me these cheques to give to the people. The names I could not read so this man told me how to say them. I think one of the names was Rosa in English. To him it was strange that the government trusted me with cheques to give to these people. There is more to the dream but not much. Like after the man helped me I still had trouble with the names and I went to the back that was like a police station and the female officer was telling me something about when I get to this place to like do all I can quickly and get out of there or I would get arrested or something. The dream is all fine and dandy but why give me a black book with names and cheques? People this dream concerns me because for me this is death. I was given death to give to these people. Yes it could be something different, but for me writing's on paper with people's name usually mean death especially cheques. So why give me death to give to a nation Lovey?

Oh man what am I missing when it comes to this dream?

I refuse to give anyone over to death. The job of death is the job of death and it truly has nothing to do with me. I see death and I tell you about death. **_So maybe this is a warning sign for Russians. If they don't amend their dirty ways and or if the Government of Russia does not amend their dirty ways; death is going to come upon the people of this land._**

Family, my true family, I truly do not know. But something is so not right with the government of this land. _You cannot give your people death because Lovey, Good God and Allelujah gave no one death to kill their land and people by._ **_As a government you cannot say you are governing your people and take their rights away from them._** No government slept with their citizens to create a child; thus no man or woman including child in government have the *right to* **CURSE AND CONDEMN THEIR LAND AND PEOPLE TO HELL BECAUSE THEY (THE GOVERNMENT) CANNOT LIVE RIGHT NOR CAN THEY GOVERN RIGHT.**

THE FUNDAMENTAL NECESSITIES OF YOUR CITIZENS IS NOT WAR, SO WHAT GIVES ANYONE OF YOU THE RIGHT AND POWER TO TAX YOUR CITIZENS TO FUND YOUR WAR CRIMES; EVILS?

YOU SWORE TO PROTECT YOUR PEOPLE AND HELP THEM; SO TRULY HELP THEM.

THERE IS A GLOBAL DESTRUCTION THAT IS COMING AND IT'S TRULY NOT GOING TO BE PRETTY.

HUMANITY IS GOING TO LOSE IT ALL EXCEPT FOR THE CHOSEN FEW. SO IF YOU AS GOVERNMENTS DON'T SMARTEN UP THEN CHARGES MUST BE LAID AGAINST ALL OF YOU GLOBALLY FOR WAR CRIMES AND BREACH OF CONTRACT.

YES SOME OF YOU HAVE THESE CHARGES LAID AGAINST YOU ALREADY, BUT FOR THOSE WHO DON'T ENSURE YOU START PREPARING FOR YOUR CITIZENS BECAUSE MANY ON LAND IS GOING TO HAVE HELL TO PAY; DIE.

Know that this breach of contract has nothing to do with man but has all to do with life. Once this contract is issued there is absolutely nothing any of you can do about it. For billions of you this contract has been issued without the war crimes. Therefore, Death must walk and take what truly belongs to them.

THIS IS NOAH'S ARK, THE TIME OF NOAH AND YOU HAVE TO PREPARE YOURSELF AS OF NOW. I WILL NOT WARN AGAIN. THE EXODUS FOR LOVEY'S PEOPLE MUST BEGIN SO THAT THE REST OF YOU CAN FACE YOUR HELL HERE ON EARTH AND IN HELL LITERALLY.

Thus the separation has been commissioned. This is the final stage and stages of man; humans.

Thus the scientists globally had better start watching the tectonic plates I've mention because I truly don't want to go to Guam.

Damn sometimes I feel like the bloody death angel. So this dream I am so going to watch and see. Hey I could be wrong and the Russian Government is going to start manning up and start looking after their old and young people. Maybe they are going to cut back on Aries – military funding and start taking care of their people like they are suppose to.

Yes I know this is wishful thinking people but you know what, it does not hurt to dream and hope for the best when it comes to these militant leaders globally. Leaders that have no good will for the lifestyle and dignity of their *people. Leaders that think by stirring up war and murdering other people makes them a superpower.*

Yes warmongers that have no respect for human and animal life including earthly life; that of mother earth.

Tell me something Lovey, how can a country and or a nation call themselves superpowers and they are broker than a church mouse? Their national debt load is in the hundreds of billions and trillions including billions.

Your land is broke and the people are homeless; suffering and you call yourself a superpower.

Nigger get a life, your land be broke. Who the hell respects you?

Well say that to my face I have weapons. Kiss my natural brown ass. So what if you have weapons. Can you eat them?

Can these weapons feed your poor and homeless?

Can these weapons provide shelter and food for your starving and malnourished including sickly and dying people?

So talk to me when you have a life and clue when it comes to life.

I am so not afraid of you because when it's all said and done; you're all bitches for death. Death is going to walk on your land and claim you.

Death is going to detonate all the weapons in your land and claim your land and people.

NONE OF YOU IS STRONGER THAN DEATH.

WHEN YOU ARE ALL GONE; LIFE AND DEATH WILL STILL BE HERE.

So you're all powerless because no matter what you do to flesh you cannot do to spirit.

It's your evil spirit that takes your evil and wicked ass to hell.

It's your wicked and evil spirit that hand you over to death and the demons of hell.

Thus many of you fight death when you see the hell you're going to face in the final stages of your life.

Oh man are the demons of hell going to have a field day with the lots of you.

Woo Nelly I so don't want to be any of you that call yourselves leaders; leaders that suppress and mistreat your citizens; rob them of their life and dignity.

Wow because I can see the smile on the faces of the demons of hell. You think your life is good and all is going to be well in Hell. Well remember Eve and how she got locked out.

Remember the people of Noah and how they got locked out. So yeah, things have not changed when it comes to the evil and wicked ways of man; humans. Hence I truly don't want to be any of you.

Yes it's sad we have no good will for each other globally thus the separation truly comes and humans are going to wail literally.

Trust me there is something happening and I cannot make heads of tails of it when it comes to the tectonic plates of earth. Everything is connecting so all of earth will be affected somehow.

No I am so not going to bust my brains over this nor will concern myself too much. I know Lovey's people will be where they are suppose to be before all hell breaks loose on earth.

And no I cannot bust my brain trying to figure the four rivers that ran from the Garden of Eden because in truth,

Lovey would not built his perfect garden and dare let evil come into it to destroy it. Thus life as we know it to me, is not good but evil.

Thus earth itself is the Garden of Eden. It matters not the land it is in because Earth was one mass of land and as time went on, the atmosphere of earth changed.

As humans evolve and become more wicked; evil, we lose more land mass. Thus humans cannot correlate their evils and wickedness to the loss of land and yes people here on earth. Thus our sins take away from all life including the life of earth in this sense.

So for now I will leave things as is and move on to book fifteen.

Michelle

So as I close this book I have to think about the dream I had this morning September 15 with my uncle's brother. I dreamt they had a feast; celebration and my uncle's brother was wearing glasses and dancing around. He was showing off in some way and I felt uncomfortable. The celebration turned into his wife ending up in the hospital and on the table you could see this bigger than a square baking pan of sweet potato pudding, but for you who are not from the Caribbean, you say sweet potato pie. In the middle portion to the edge you could see the cut, well I could see the cut going from the outer edge of the center of the table. The cut looked like a goal post cut if that makes any sense. She had been having headaches lately in the dream. I don't know what happened after that but I saw my doctor who was white and I asked him to look at her paper work; hospital records. People please do not ask me how I got her hospital records but I did. My uncle's brother's wife was in the room and for the life of me I could not remember my own doctor's name. I ended up introducing him like this. Christine meet my doctor and my doctor this is Christine. Did I get chastised?

Man did he chastise me for the introduction. Any ho, he looked at her paperwork and or the hospital records and was shocked that they were giving her the drug they were giving her. I believe in the dream the drug is classed as a Htmp and or an Hmp drug. I know the drug in the dream was a Hydrochloride drug and or one of the H drugs. Listen I so do not know anything about pharmaceutical drugs and so not going to get involved in pharmaceuticals when it comes to drugs. And knowing me I am probably going to in another book.

It's really weird also that in the dream, my doctor was beginning to forget things. Suffice it to say, we did not get far in the discussion of my uncle's brother's wife chart. Our conversation was interrupted by a female white nurse and he had to go; was whisked away.

Weird because this is the second doctor now I am dreaming that is forgetting things. Wow.

I'm forgetting things too. Wow.

So, I am missing something in the medical field and or the health and welfare of my family in Jamaica.

I am going to have to get a calling card to warn my uncle of the medications they are giving his wife. I also have to warn my uncle's brother's wife to be careful of any meds she is taking. And yes I have to safeguard myself with the drugs I am taking.

Listen people I have the wobbly wobblies and I am trying folate to see if that helps. I tried it once, this dollar store brand and I felt different. Mind you my urine baffled me so I am going to go to the health food store and or Wal-Mart and get a proper bottle of folate. But it's weird though, why are doctors going to start forgetting things?

Is selective memory loss going to be the in thing when it comes to pharmaceuticals and the pharmaceutical industry?

Who knows but we will certainly find out. Listen fam, in this book I am so not putting a lot of emphasis on anything a part from the tectonic plates I've mentioned above.

Lovey want his house in the Cayman Islands but it's weird because the Cayman Islands is slap dab in the pathway of the Caribbean tectonic plate. So this makes no sense to me especially when this white man in one of my visions told me that Jamaica is going to be destroyed. I know, I know Jamaica is on the list of places to be destroyed and up till now eee caane happen yet. Weird

So if Jamaica is going to be destroyed what about the Cayman Islands?

They are in close proximity to each other and two people are saying the Cayman Islands is going to be destroyed. I did not see destruction for Cayman. You know what, let me close this book and leave things alone because I cannot see all thus I know not all.

Lovey works in mysterious ways. Hey, destruction may be for one but not the other. I will not go on a panic attack for the Cayman Islands. He said one thing and it's his thing I have to go by.

I know destruction cometh, and to me the Cocos Plate and the Eurasian Plate are the ones to watch along with the Arabian Plate. Not so much the Arabian Plate but more so the Eurasian Plate and this is due to my Air France dream and or vision.

Exact illustration of goal post cut in my dream. This picture taken from the internet and no copyright infringement intended and never will be intended.

So everyone truly enjoy because if I continue with this book I am going to be super confused.

So how is your day going so far?

Do hope it's going great and if it isn't, turn your cheek.

Did you?

Yes.

Hey, I am so kissing you.

Always remember, you are important so truly love you and do you. Hey people are going to look and stare when you dress differently.

Hey, they will call you loud when you laugh loud.

They will look and stare at your underwear in that see through dress or skirt.

Hey, remember the funky blue and green hair. They will stare even drop their jaw.

Just be you because no one else can be you no matter how hard they try.

You are one of a kind and yes some twins are one of a kind also.

SO AS I DEDICATE FREE YOURSELF BY ALBOROSIE TO YOU. Truly "love you before you love someone else." You are truly important thus live good and free.

Michelle

Man I am opening this book because I am so pissed this morning. I do not know why I keep changing my mandate for leaving my children. I truly can't do this anymore because I am not getting anywhere. I am getting stressed out and angry. It's not my future but theirs, and it seems I want better for my children more than them.

I've noticed when the doors are closed they are so closed to me and I refuse to knock any down. I've tried and failed and so it will stand when it comes to these books. I never knew there could be so many closed doors that a sealed tight when it comes to me and these books.

*In the spiritual realm all is closed to me when it comes to my own people and frankly I truly don't give a damn. So Lovey, **stop constantly showing me that I will not be accepted by the Black Race both male and female.** I am no different from you in this sense. So stop showing me and or reminding me of the rejection I will get from my own globally. You are rejected and so am I, there is no difference in this when it comes to us. I've told you time and time again, if a people don't want you leave them the hell alone. I am learning to do this with my own. Yes I give them books but it is going to stop because most black don't help blacks, **and in truth I AM NOT LOOKING FOR ANYTHING FROM THEM (THE BLACK RACE).** They cannot say I did not try with them when it comes to these books. They are the ones that refuse to open doors for you, me and the black community. So I too must leave them the hell alone.*

I refuse handouts; hence I look for no handouts from the Black Community. I do me.

I cannot force anyone to accept the truth of Life and Death especially life because billions have and has chosen death for self. And yes I refuse to force anyone to accept the truth. It is not my right to do so. Thus if billions including my family reject me so be it. As long as I am safe and away from them all when this massive destruction comes, I am truly good to go because I am depending on you to hide me and our good and true seeds from them (the left behinds).

They chose death; so let them go with death come on now.

THUS AS A NATION OF PEOPLE (BLACK PEOPLE) WE LIVE IN DISUNITY AND ANYONE CAN FOOL US WITH THEIR CRAP AND BAGS OF LIES. Therefore, I have no time for foolishness. I am too old for crap and the stupid things some of us as black people do. If the black race want to continue to go to the slaughter house with death, who the hell am I to stop them. Let them go because as MARCUS MOSIAH GARVEY SAID, "A people without the knowledge of their past history, origin and culture is like a tree without roots."

"If you have no confidence in self, you are twice defeated in the race of life. With confidence, you have won even before you have started."

"Liberate the minds of men and ultimately you will liberate the bodies of men."

So no, I will not fight anyone for their acceptance of death because we the black race have and has lost our roots. And no matter how Lovey tries to show us this, we cannot see it.

*Like I said, when we accept religions, cultures, languages, customs, rites and names of other nations; we've lost our true identity. We've given up all that is ours to be assimilated into another man's culture. Thus we are not known anymore. When we are assimilated and or colonized; other nations can say we did not exist. **We were never in that land because our name is now their name.***

Our language is now their language.

Their customs and rights are now our customs and rights.

Their religion and religions of nastiness is now our religion and religions of nastiness.

Our dress is now their dress.

Their people is now our people because we marry into their nastiness and accept their nasty sex; sexual practice that say, it's okay to procreate with family members. *Thus the nasty and filthy book that they give us globally called the Holy Bible. This is the book of nastiness and sin thus I call it the book of death because it is dead; from death. Thus in revelations it tells you those that follow after Jesus (Zeus and or Heysuis) are the first begotten of* *the dead. So to me I worry not about my race. Wi too damn falla batty. WE GIVE UP OUR OWN TO FOLLOW THE DEVIL'S OWN. So truly, I worry not about my own. THE LIES WE AS THE BLACK RACE ACCEPT ARE THE LIES THAT WILL NOW KILL US. MANY HAVE AND HAS DIED; THUS MANY ARE SEALED IN HELL AND CANNOT COME OUT. And don't even look at me because I will not go into hell and dirty myself for any. Stay the hell in hell because wi too damn fool fool an licky licky. Thus many follow di careless Ethiopians to dem grave. Nuff di figet cause granny and some mumma reminded us of the careless Ethiopians back in the days of old.*

People a lead wi to wi grave anna dat wi a falla an sey wey dem sey a di truth. Not one of us got off our lazy ass and said, "Gad, how can this book be the truth when a pure perversion of nastiness; family ram business inna it?

Wi nuh sey Gad, yu accept murder?

Wi nuh sey Gad, the commandment sey thou shalt not kill, but yu dey pan battlefield with David a kill? Isn't that a double standard on your part?

How can you say do not kill but yet kill?

Wha kine a crasses dat dey.

Yu liad den. Yu caane tell us one thing and do another. Are you not confusing us?

Yes I see you trying Lovey and still we as a nation of people, still sit under the crap that they feed and tell us. Instead of continuing with innovation and our powerful thinking, we get boxed in and become a part of the psychological game of thrones and thorns and I refuse to be like this. I refuse to let people think for me because I can do and I do do for myself.

I don't want to be a part of the spiritual collective of losers anymore Lovey.

Do not control my spirit anymore because I am truly not free when you do this. So yes, I am breaking free of your shackles and chains Lovey and I am letting go of your collective. I truly do not need you to control my spirit. I was born free thus I have to be free in the physical and spiritual realm. I don't need you controlling me and my thoughts because in truth, I am not getting anywhere with you.

I cannot control you nor do I want to control you.

Like I said, I refuse to tell anyone to accept you because as humans we are to know better.

I refuse to give anyone religions of men to continue to kill themselves by. I am not a part of the death collective; thus I relinquish the Collective of Life because I am truly not free. Life does not cage anyone and no one should cage my spirit and hold my spirit captive to them. I freely give of me to you Lovey, but in all that I freely give, you give pain and heartache. Thus all I give back to you including these books.

I will no longer fight with you and for you for your best interest because in truth, you've allowed this mess to continue on for far too long. Instead of fixing it (all) properly, you've left us broken and confused like you and this is truly wrong.

You cannot give life and give it half assed; without truth.

Thus my dreams this morning and my son who pissed me off because he cannot wake up properly for school. I cannot do anymore for my children.

You heard what my daughter asked me about RESP. Why I did not start it when they were younger. But could I Lovey around their father? Thus Behind the Scars that I cannot look upon or correct. Nor will I have a book two. You know my struggles and heartache, and if I do get readers for these books they will see my heartache and pain.

<u>Life is corrupted Lovey thus good life cannot be found on earth and you know this. THUS WE AS HUMANS ARE LIFE'S VIRUS THAT IT CANNOT GET RID OF.</u>

We as humans pollute and contaminate everything.

You know this but yet you are not willing to give us your antivirus formula. No wait, Death is the antivirus formula that billions of us will have to face shortly.

Thus my dreams this morning were crazy people and I had to open this book and vent.

Dreamt the now Prime Minister of Jamaica and she had grey and black hair; salt and pepper hair. I did not say anything to her because she looked sad. So I left things alone. Thus that was that dream.

I also dreamt I was in this place. It wasn't a church but the setting was like a church. Somehow I felt I was high up, so I am going to leave it at high up due to feel. In the dream I was preaching to black males and females. I was telling them about God and I started to say Lovey and I explained to the crowd, not a big crowd but small crowd that I call God Lovey. In the dream while preaching some people left, they did not like what I was preaching. And that was that dream.

I also dreamt about my brother and Margaret and I so have to give them a call to see how they are doing.

Dreamt I said I am going to take a trip and my sister said she is coming and we went as a family. On the way back from the trip and or vacation, my children left the plane without me and I could not find my hand luggage anywhere. Fam, I looked everywhere for my luggage but could not find it. I found my daughter's bag and other pieces of luggage, but could not find mine. I found my clothes but no luggage. My hand luggage was gone just leaving my clothes. My last child somehow came back and he was helping me but he too could not find my hand luggage. So I figured my other children took my luggage. I went into this area and my sister and her friend were there and my sister made a comment and or was telling her friend something about me. I told her not to talk my business to people. When I said that my sister was not pleased and (her attitude) ticked me off; she continued with her telling tales of me. She went up to this one particular black stewardess and was telling lies about me and it infuriated me; so much that I told her we were done as sisters. I never want to see her again and left where she was. The same stewardess came up to me and told me where she saw a lot of suitcases. She said Portia (the now Prime Minister of Jamaica) has a lot of suitcases (luggage) and I told her; not even if they paid me all the money in the world would I take a suitcase from her. And Lovey forgive me if this dream is not in order of flowetry when it comes to the sequences of the dream.

Dreamt I was waiting for an elevator. The elevator was broken but I got on and these people got on. One white lady and her man that I believe was black and two black females. I can't remember if one was selling things but we got off at the top level. The white lady and her man got off and so did I along with the two young looking black females. We started to talk about religion. One of the lady stayed and listened but the other one left citing she reads the bible and the bible was her choice. And that was the end of that dream.

I can't remember if I saw the destruction of Jamaica but Death; you are duly warned. Stop toying with me when it comes to Jamaica because I am so not in the mood. You like to play too damned much when it comes to my homeland. I told you before stop bleeping toying with me when it comes to this land. You have to do what you have to do and I will not stop you, so stop bleeping around.

You have a job to do so damn well do it and don't look to me for permission. The door and window have and has been closed to this land when it comes to Lovey long ago. I am the one that is holding on for some strange reason. I will not fight you for people who cares nothing for self and land. Walk because it is your right. I've stepped aside already and I will not commission Lovey for the people there. ***I truly love the land, but I do not truly love the wicked and evil people of that land.*** *Lovey gave us his name, his Breath of Life, his flag of life and all the people did was destroy them all and for this there is no forgiveness in my book.*

We made a pledge and I too did make a pledge to him and I am honouring him the best I can. But I cannot be a part of his collectiveness of spiritual control. I can no longer allow him to let you Death and your wicked and evil spirits and people get to me. So truly stop lest I take it all from you for real literally. I know this is what you want thus I will not give a Babylonian a way in. It's truly not going to work with me but nice try.

Like I said Lovey and will forever tell you. I will not fight anyone for religion. Black people of all colour and creed and sort can kiss my natural brown ass when it comes to them and their religions of men. I do not sell religion nor will I give you religion of NASTY PERVERTS THAT WRITE BOOKS OF LIES BASED ON NASTINESS AND GIVE TO ANYONE.

From beginning to end they give you family ram business thus many of us in society thinks it's okay to shag family.

Father shagging daughter and brother shagging sister and this you are okay with. I grew up in a society where this is normal for some and it's not right. Family do procreate with family members and this is not right. **THUS I ASK YOU**

AND WILL FOREVER ASK YOU. IF WE GET FALSE TEACHINGS AND LIES TO LIVE BY, WILL WE NOT DO ALL THAT IS WRONG AND SINFUL IN THY SIGHT?

Will we not live like the nasty and filthy?

Will we not condemn ourselves like the nasty and filthy?

Lies are all we have Lovey and this is what we live by.

You made it so by stepping aside. And yes I know what you are trying to tell me, but if you are not listening to me, and if you are not hearing me, why the hell should I stay with you? You make it hard for your people; so why should we live in hardship an den tun roune haffi bi di sacrifice of evil? Thus this brings me to the dream I forget where my own black people was seeking me to kill me.

Like I said, we kill for lies thus lies is what we live by. I refuse to be like the rest of the world Lovey because, "TRUTH IS EVERLASTING LIFE." WITHOUT TRUTH NO ONE CAN LIVE AND IT'S THE TRUTH THAT IS KEEPING ME GOING. IT'S THE TRUTH THAT'S KEEPING THIS PLANET GOING AND THAT TRUTH IS YOU DESPITE MY WAYS WITH YOU. Thus yet again I am missing something on the ground and in the air. But what am I missing Lovey?

I've talked about the tectonic plates. Are there more plates that I am missing? I told you, I truly do not want to go to

Guam because it's a US held territory and you know just how nasty and filthy the United States of America is. They've condemned self thus the separation of lands must take place. <u>YOU HAVE TO SEPARATE GOOD FROM EVIL.</u>

HE DID NOT FINISH HIS JOB SO TRULY COMPLETE IT. I KNOW FOR A FACT THAT MOSES DID NOT SEPARATE THE RED SEA; HE DID. HE IS ETHIOPIAN BECAUSE HE CONTROLS THE SEAS; ELEMENTS. HE MUST COMPLETE THE SEPARTIONS BECAUSE ALL ENCIRCLES EACH OTHER AND ALL ARE CONNECTED. SO HE MUST BRING ABOUT THE FINAL SEPARATION. I CANNOT DO THIS FOR HIM BECAUSE IT WAS HIM YOU ORDAINED TO DO THIS IN THE FIRST PLACE.

I will not dirty my hands for anyone not even you Lovey. So please do that which is right and not which is wrong.

Humans did let you go and you have to live with this. We sacrificed self to evil.

<u>**We gave up our rights to evil.**</u> Yes we did wrong, <u>**but that does not change the fact that we did choose and that choice was not you for billions.**</u>

Also, what is this yellow bucket with dirty water that I saw a hand in in my waking moments with eyes closed?

Yes I know my hallway needs to be cleaned but I know otherwise.

Listen I refuse to put my hands in dirty water. I will not dirty my hands for you or anyone. So if you think I am going to dirty my hands for you, you had better truly think again because I am not doing it. You as father and mother made your mess; you clean it because I am tired of talking to you. I am not your maid nor are you mine. You as father and mother cannot leave everything for me to fix. What you can fix fix it because I am tired. I need to mend and fix the issues in my life and one of those issues is finding a place and doing for me not you.

I cannot wait at your doorstep anymore to receive jobs from you. I am tired and I need to do for me now. You don't listen to me so why should I stay? So since you are my hand luggage and or suitcase and I will be searching for you when you are gone then so be it. You do not scare me because I am not leaving you for leaving you sake. You don't listen and I am tired of you not listening to me.

Yes my greatest fear is losing you but not anymore. I have to live with my decision so stop. I know you are telling me I cannot do without you and in fact I truly can't, so truly listen.

I know you are saying I cannot leave my children also, but I have to and you are hindering me and I truly don't like it. I cannot live in a household where I have to constantly protect children that are not listening.

Listen Lovey, I can't live with my second child anymore. He hardly works and when I give him phone numbers of places that are hiring he tells me not to give him these numbers because he knows what he's doing. He's told me he never listens to me; so why should I sit with a child that refuses to listen. It's the same with me and you. Why should I sit with a father and mother that truly do not listen?

No one can live like this. I know I can't and you truly can't hence the story of Eve (Evening).

I know the consequence (s) of life in regards to the bad decisions I make; but what about my life Lovey?

How important is my life to you?
How much do you truly love me?
What have you sacrificed for me?

Yes I went there because you know you are my good and bad everything.

Listen, I've told you, if a man or woman including child don't want you, leave them the hell alone.

I cannot and I will not fight with black people and or the black race for you.

I will not fight with my children for what's best for them anymore.

I will not fight and battle you for my health and sanity; best interest anymore.

I will not fight with them (my children and the black race) for the betterment of self because I am waiting for the day you tell me to slam the door hard in their faces because we don't listen. We readily accept lies over truth.

WHEN WE GET THE TRUTH WE DON'T WANT IT. WE REFUSE IT AND THIS IS WHY SATAN AND OR THE DEVIL CAN PUT IM POT PAN FIYA AN WITHIN A NANOSECOND; NO, LESS THAN A NANOSECOND WE THE BLACK RACE GIVE YOU LOVEY UP FOR HIM SATAN AND OR THE DEVIL. THIS IS WHY YOU SHOWED ME HELL IS FULL OF BLACK PEOPLE AND RECRUITING MORE.

We will always sell you out Lovey for dirty pieces of silver.

Thus I more than over stand the Jesus sell out code. Thus in the spiritual realm you constantly show me Blacks; my own will never help me. I have to fix things on my own and I am tired of it. As women we have a hard time with men. We will always be used and abused and I am fed up. Thus I am going to listen to Etana and step out of Babylon and into my own new and good, honest and true; truly peaceful mountain; land of true peace and harmony that is abundant in positive energy and prosperity. THIS IS THE NEW MOUNT ZION THAT IS MADE BY ME; MY TRUE TRUTH AND MORE THAN UNCONDITIONAL LOVE OF TRUTH.

No not your loving so Lovey, but my more than true and good unconditional love of more than truth. This truth you cannot comprehend Lovey because you leave me barren and shackled and chain. I do not want or need to be in your shackles anymore. So truly release my from your bondage so that I can truly live free and good; truthful and whole the way my good and true life was meant to be.

I cannot continue to give you my victory Lovey because at the end of the day, you see the ills and wickedness of man; humanity and have and has truly done nothing constructive to fix the issues that are plaguing us.

It's not just humans that are suffering, earth and my waterways are suffering. <u>THUS I FOUND THE SONG BLACK WOMAN</u> ON THE INTERNET <u>BY JUDY MOWAT.</u> *Thus I wrote these lines.*

SOME OF US AS BLACK WOMAN NEED TO LISTEN TO THIS SONG (Black Woman by Judy Mowat) BECAUSE FOR TOO LONG WE'VE BEEN SHACKLED AND CHAINED;

ABUSED AND REFUSED. YES I AM ONE OF THEM THAT HAVE BEEN ABUSED AND REFUSED, BUT I HOLD MY HEAD UP HIGH; MOVE ON AND DO ALL TO WALK UPRIGHT AND STRONG. I DO ALL TO COME OUT OF MY STRUGGLES. I KNOW MY STRENGTH; SO I WILL NOT BE BROKEN ANYMORE. I AM MENDED; FIXED; WHOLE.

I WILL CARRY ON UNTIL BETTER COMES BECAUSE I AM WOMAN; A STRONG BLACK WOMAN.

So in all I do Lovey, I thank you and you will never be forgotten. I must rise and you've shown me I must rise on my own. I will because each day I rise, I am thankful in some way to be alive.

I am thankful that I have you protecting me. Thus my protection I will always leave in your hands. And although we cannot be together, you will always remain in my heart with me because despite it all; you are my true love. So whatever comes come, but you must let the final separation happen and you must allow and or give your good and true people passage in the good and true land and lands you've ordained for them. Plenty and or an abundance of good and organic, true organic food and water, trees must they have to keep them sheltered from the brutal storm that is coming. Father and Lovey, you must do this for me because the good seeds you've given me I know are your books but I've made those good seeds the readers; my true family that reads these books and have adhered to life. Meaning they've started to amend their ways.

No Babylonians Lovey because you've shown me them.
I refuse them; thus I refuse sins wicked and evil people. Also, I will not clash with my family, so whatever lies they want to spread let them do it. Let them talk if dem want to because I saw the lies beforehand.

I will not conform to them (the lies of my family). So let dem talk because when the boomerang comes tumbling down when I get pissed; know Lovey that there will be no getting up for them. So whatever family member is going to start with their lies, know that I will not sit down and take it lightly.

No, I will not pick up weapons because when mi cuss I know the devil and the demons of hell quinge. So I worry not about them.

I will not worry about you too Lovey because you now have to truly leave the Black Race alone and I've told you this.

You cannot continue to try to save people that don't want you to save them.

You cannot continue to provide a home and or shelter for people who continually RAT YOU OUT; CHOOSE THE DEVIL AND OR SATAN OVER YOU.

TRUST LOVEY; THUS I WENT TO THE TOP OF YOUR MOUNTAIN AND DID NOT LIKE IT AT THE TOP. THUS MY CHOICE IS THE FIRST LEVEL OF LIFE. YES I CAN GO UP AND DOWN THE MOUNTAIN BUT NATURE, WATER AND THE TREES ARE MY TRUE STAY AND YOU HAVE TO PROTECT THEM ALSO. It's not humans alone that have life and it seems you've forgotten this.

A tree never sold you out for dirty pieces of silver, but humans globally have.

The waterways shine and clean pathways for us humans and no waterway have ever sold you out for dirty pieces of silver, but humans cannot say otherwise. We sell you out to death. So truly think where your priorities lie when it comes to nature as well.

Humans are not the only ones involved in this. Thus nature sin not, but humans cannot say the same.

Human sell you out every chance they get so truly think.
Do that which is right for nature; the environment; earth.

When all is gone away Lovey, Life will still be around. Thus I truly worry not about You because You will always be there.

Evil cannot take from your life Lovey, I know this.

*Evil has and have taken from the lives of humans, **but at the end of the day, that one good tree will remain with you, because that one good tree is your lifeline; an extension of you.** **Know that you will always have true life in me thus take my good tree of life and truly plant it beside your good tree. Let it grow with you because I do trust you with all of me.***

Hopefully one day our good and true people will do the same; plant their good and true tree beside you.

Never forget my beautiful mother, Rosalind Rosetta Morgan. Tomorrow is her birthday. Happy birthday Miss Peggy. As your birthday comes, I thank you for giving me the strength to carry on even an my weakest days; hours.

Lovey thank you for giving me more than a blessed queen in earth and in the spiritual realm.

Michelle

OTHER BOOKS BY MICHELLE JEAN

Blackman Redemption – The Fall of Michelle Jean
Blackman Redemption – After the Fall Apology
Blackman Redemption – World Cry – Christine Lewis
Blackman Redemption
Blackman Redemption – The Rise and Fall of Jamaica
Blackman Redemption – The War of Israel
Blackman Redemption – The Way I Speak to God
Blackman Redemption – A Little Talk With Man
Blackman Redemption – The Den of Thieves
Blackman Redemption – The Death of Jamaica
Blackman Redemption – Happy Mother's Day
Blackman Redemption – The Death of Faith
Blackman Redemption – The War of Religion
Blackman Redemption – The Death of Russia
Blackman Redemption – The Truth
Blackman Redemption – Spiritual War
Blackman Redemption – The Youths
Blackman Redemption – Black Man Where Is Your God?

The New Book of Life
The New Book of Life – A Cry For The Children
The New Book of Life – Judgement
The New Book of Life – Love Bound
The New Book of Life – Me
The New Book of Life – Life

Just One of Those Days
Book Two – Just One of Those Days
Just One of Those Days – Book Three The Way I Feel
Just One of Those Days – Book Four

The Days I Am Weak
Crazy Thoughts – My Book of Sin
Broken
Ode to Mr. Dean Fraser

A Little Little Talk
A Little Little Talk – Book Two

Prayers
My Collective
A Little Talk/A Time For Fun and Play
Simple Poems
Behind The Scars
Songs of Praise And Love

Love Bound
Love Bound – Book Two

Dedication Unto My Kids
More Talk
Saving America From A Woman's Perspective
My Collective the Other Side of Me
My Collective the Dark Side of Me
A Blessed Day
Lose To Win
My Doubtful Days – Book One

My Little Talk With God
My Little Talk With God – Book Two

A Different Mood and World – Thinking

My Nagging Day
My Nagging Day – Book Two

Friday September 13, 2013
My True Love
It Would Be You
My Day

A Little Advice – Talk
1313, 2032, 2132 – The End of Man
Tata

MICHELLE'S BOOK BLOG – BOOKS 1 – 20

My Problem Day
A Better Way
Stay – Adultery and the Weight of Sin – Cleanliness
Message

Let's Talk
Lonely Days – Foundation
A Little Talk With Jamaica – As Long As I Live
Instructions For Death
My Lonely Thoughts
My Lonely Thoughts – Book Two
My Morning Talks – Prayers With God
What A Mess
My Little Book
A Little Word With You
My First Trip of 2015
Black Mother – Mama Africa
Islamic Thought
My California Trip January 2015
My True Devotion by Michelle – Michelle Jean
My Many Questions To God
My Talk
My Talk Book Two

My Talk Book Three – The Rise of Michelle Jean
My Talk Book Four
My Talk Book Five
My Talk Book Six
My Talk Book Seven
My Talk Book Eight – My Depression
My Talk Book Nine – Death
My Talk Book Ten – Wow
My Day – Book Two
My Talk Book Eleven – What About December?
Haven Hill
What About December – Book Two
My Talk Book Twelve – Summary and or Confusion
My Talk Book Thirteen